'WE THE PEOPLE'

'WE THE PEOPLE'

A Pictorial Celebration Of America

By The Winners Of The Parade-Fuji National Photo Contest
Introduction By Walter Anderson
Continuum • New York

1988

The Continuum Publishing Company
370 Lexington Avenue
New York, NY 10017

Library of Congress Cataloging-in-Publication Data
We the people: a pictorial celebration of America
by the winners of the Parade-Fuji National Photo Contest:
introduction by Walter Anderson.
p.   cm.
ISBN 0-8264-0405-7
1. Ethnology—United States—Pictorial works.
2. United States—Social life and customs—1971—Pictorial works.
I. Fuji Photo Film U.S.A.
II. Parade (New York, N.Y.)
E184. A1W325 1988
779′ .9306′ 0973—dc 19   87-36089 CIP

Grateful acknowledgment is made to Houghton Mifflin Company
for permission to quote from "The Congressional Liberty"
in THE COMPLETE POETICAL WORKS OF AMY LOWELL.
Copyright © 1955 by Houghton Mifflin Company.
Copyright © 1983 renewed by Houghton Mifflin Company,
Brinton P. Roberts, Esquire and G. D'Andelot Belin, Esquire.
Reprinted by permission of
Houghton Mifflin Company.

▶
Migrant workers in a
tomato field outside of
Homestead, Fla. Photo
by Allen Chinitz of
Ridgewood, N.J.

Introduction

When *Parade* magazine was established nearly half a century ago, its original designation was as a weekly "Picture Magazine."

I'm glad that this description was soon dropped, for *Parade*, which is read by more than 65 million Americans each week, has become far more than an assemblage of photos. Its articles touch on all phases of human activity and thought; its writers include outstanding authors and journalists, as well as national and international leaders.

But pictures remain integral to its purpose and function, for they, too, tell who we are and what we think. So it was natural for *Parade*'s editors to hit upon the idea of a photo contest when we were seeking a way in which our readers could join in celebrating the Bicentennial of the U.S. Constitution. Our theme was "We the People," and how better could we present a cross-section of our country as it is viewed by Americans today? In collaboration with Fuji Photo Film U.S.A., we invited our readers—amateurs no less than professionals—to submit their favorite photos illustrating the theme of "We the People."

We expected a heavy response, of course, but what we actually received astonished us—some 130,000 entries from every state in the Union, with many of such high quality that our project manager, Brent Petersen, and our panel of distinguished judges, the author Alex Haley, the photographer Eddie Adams, the psychologist Joyce Brothers, and the director of "Action," Donna M. Alvarado, had great difficulty in selecting the 100 best.

Perhaps we really shouldn't have been so surprised. We live in a visual age, when taking pictures has become almost a national pastime. From the days of the Daguerreotype to the home video era, Americans have excelled at photography, and the heightened sophistication of camera equipment in recent years has been more than matched by a growth in technical know-how and artistic ambition on the part of camera users.

So the pictures in this book will give you an idea of both the artistry and the technique which amateur American photographers—those who take pictures for fun rather than for profit—bring to their favorite pastime. Many of these pictures, I firmly believe, could hang in photo exhibits—indeed, they all are a part of a permanent exhibit honoring the Bicentennial of the Constitution that was first shown in Philadelphia September 13-19, 1987.

But apart from their sheer worth as photographs, I believe that they go far toward capturing the spirit of this country today. There is an affirmative quality to them that, to my mind, represents our people's true qualities and feelings as we approach the end of the decade of the 1980s.

Judging by their variety, one gets the impression that practically everybody in this country travels about with a camera in pocket, purse or knapsack, or suspended by a strap around the neck. By far, the majority of these pictures have an improvisational, spur-of-the-moment quality that gives them a freshness and spontaneity that often eludes the most skilled professionals.

Predictably, some of the photos show Americans at play—visiting amusement parks, joining in sports, enjoying hobbies. But interestingly, many of the photographers found themselves taking pictures of Americans at work—railroaders, sheep breeders, storekeepers, even migrant field-hands. It's as if we wanted to show that we are an industrious people, and we believe that beauty is to be found in the workplace as readily as it is elsewhere.

The home and family are frequent subjects. Some of the pictures in this book raise the practice of taking snapshots of the kids to the realm of high art. A toddler in the bathtub, a boy in the barber's chair, kids wandering around the family farm—all these turn out to make for worthy, and even memorable subject matter. Many of these pictures were taken by the youngsters' parents, brothers, sisters or other family members.

The enormous ethnic variety of America is also reflected in these photos. The broad span of racial groups, from the original American Indians to the latest wave of arrivals from the Far East, attracted the sympathetic interest of the photographers. At other epochs in our history, other groups might have been more widely represented—but the message that America welcomes all remains constant throughout the generations.

The place that the elderly play in American life today also is a recurrent theme. Taking snapshots of the kids no longer is the main family photographic activity; nowadays we are equally prone to take photos of Grandma and Grandpa too. Some of the most haunting pictures in this collection capture the courage and serenity which many carry into their old age.

Family, friendship, work, recreation, and the generations communicating and helping each other—these then are the basic material of everyday life in America today—the aspects that our people find closest to them, and most worthy of recording in the photographs they take.

In all likelihood, these were the same concerns that were felt by the Americans of 200 years ago—those who shaped and adopted the Constitution we still live under. Had there been cameras in those days, some remarkably similar pictures might have recorded life as it was in that bygone era.

It is good that our values remain the same and our enthusiasm has not diminished. Two hundred years ago we were a vibrant, productive and forward-looking people, and we remain so today. That was the basic meaning of the Constitutional Bicentennial, and that is also the message in these remarkable pictures that today's Americans have taken of one another.

Walter Anderson

Railroad man. Joseph Rauch, 44, a maintenance repairman, takes a break at railroad yards in Jim Thorpe, Pa. Photo by George Harvan of Lansford, Pa.

On previous page. Pals? Oh, brother. Checking the wheat for ripeness at the Sauer family farm near Loveland, Colo., are (l to r) Jacob Randolph, 2, Zachary Andrew, 3, Matthew Harrison, 5 and Joshua Caleb, 6. Photo by their mother, Gale J. Sauer.

66 We, the people of the United States,
in order to form a more perfect Union,
establish justice, insure domestic tranquility,
provide for the common defense, promote the general welfare,
and secure the blessings of liberty
to ourselves and our posterity,
do ordain and establish this Constitution for
the United States of America. 99

—Constitution of the United States

66 We, the people without a race,
Without a language;
Of all races, and of none;
Of all tongues, and one imposed;
Of all traditions and all pasts,
With no tradition and no past.
A patchwork and an altarpiece... 99

—Amy Lowell, The Congressional Liberty

Wild one? Randall Behrens, 30, riding his Harley across Wyoming en route to Sturgis, S.D. Photo, taken
from seat of second motorcycle, by Theresa Marie Hooper of Lincoln, Neb.

The Fronzolis' pool—designed, built and painted by four generations of the Fronzoli family. Photo by Tarris W. Fronzoli of Mt. Airy, Md.

American flag—"we-the-people"-style—was conceived for a celebration of family and friends at Anacostia Naval Station in Washington, D.C., on July 4, 1985. Photo by Larry Olsen of Alexandria, Va.

▶

Carlin Dunne, 4, receives career counseling from firefighter, James Scott Mackie, as Sparky looks on. Photo taken at fire station near Santa Barbara, Calif., by Barbara Jean del Valle of Santa Barbara.

◀ ◀

On previous page. New Americans. Caitlin Rose Kyung Gannon and Brynn Rose Young Gannon—adopted twin daughters of Patty and Martin Gannon of Wallingford, Conn.—on the day the 3-year-old Korean-born girls became U.S. citizens. Photo by the girls' aunt, Nancy K. Agostini of Williamstown, Mass.

For the birds? Five sea gulls perch on rail facing elderly couple on bench in Vero Beach, Fla.
Photo by Jeffrey Camp of South Daytona, Fla.

▼

Christopher Newberry, 6, in flight on a rainy
September day. Photo by his mother, Linda Newberry,
outside their home in Jermyn, Pa.

◀

Stephen Bugnaski, 6, waits for the school bus in a
winter morning mist. Photo by his father, Mark
Bugnaski, of Kingsville, Md.

John Henry Williams, 67, helps out, part-time, at the Community Grocery and Deli in Raleigh, N.C. Photo by Sadie Bridger of Raleigh.

Allison Marie Solberg, 4, runs barefoot and otherwise unhindered to her daddy along northern Oregon's Pacific coastline. Photo by father, David A. Solberg of Portland, Ore.

◀

Boy with feet. Justin
Stambuk, 2, regards
runners getting set for
Azalea Trail Run in
Mobile, Ala. Photo by his
father, Jose A. Stambuk
of Mobile.

On following page. T.
Lally Meck, 2, feeds sea
gulls at Stone Harbor in
New Jersey. Photo by his
mother, Karen Lally
Meck of Pittsburgh, Pa.

27

Mary Elizabeth Perkins, 3 months, "goes Hollywood" after completing her first trip around the block of her home. Photo by her mother, Jo Lynn of Birmingham, Ala.

Bathtime at the Luke household in Stillwater, Minn., with Melanie Ann, 4, Taylor David, 2, and Maggie Jane, 6 months. Photo by their father, Brian D. Luke.

Miss Bubbles. Two-year-old Nikko Rose takes a bubble bath at home in Plymouth, Mass. Photo by her mother, Athalyn J. Rose.

Carleigh Brunot, 3, offers comfort to little sister, Kaylan, 2, with bunny. Photo by their mother, Beth Ann Brunot of Meadville, Pa.

► Max the bulldog joins Mike Sombar in a drink on the front lawn of his home in Augusta, Ga. Photo by Suzanne Sombar of Augusta, Ga.

Ballet dancers Ali Galkin, 12, and Sherry Seling, 18, just after a recital. Photo by Marilynn Galkin of Costa Mesa, Calif., who is Ali's mother and Sherry's aunt.

"English ladies at tea"—Malea Flis, 7, and sister, Jennifer, 6, play a game of pretend in their backyard. Photo by their mother, Susan Flis of Oriskany, N.Y.

► Handicapped couple Ann Marie and Tony Scarpino Jr. on their wedding day in Burbank, Ill. Photo by Richard Berquist of Fayetteville, Ark.

▲
Woman with kite. Georgie Percy, 75, recovering from stroke, flies kite in hills of Rancho, Calif.
Photo by her husband, Virgil, 74, of Temecula, Calif.

◄
Volunteer Karen Wilson Fox (aka Raggedy Ann)
cheers 100-year-old Anna Coleman at convalescent
hospital in Santa Barbara, Calif. Photo by W. Scott
Vallance of San Diego.

In my taxi. Ryan Weideman of New York City took this picture of
himself and three passengers in his cab.

The kids get a ride. John Sumner of Atlanta, Ga., took this photo of himself behind the wheel of his pickup, with, (l to r) Terry Culver, 13, Antonio Stephen, 12, and Mary Stephen, 10, all of Kingston, Ga., in back.

▲

Arthur and Katie Schnake with Gimly on the front porch of their farm near Hoyleton, Ill. They had been married 71
years when Arthur died at 94. Photo by Joe Niederhofer of Hoyleton.

▶

On the beach. Joseph W. Lane, 72, and Lucille, 73,
of Phoenix, Ariz., once Wisconsin farmers, visit
Daytona Beach, Fla. They have been married 53 years.
Photo by Peggy S. Duhl of Ormond Beach, Fla.

In tune with time. Leon Levitch, a survivor of the Holocaust, tunes a piano. Photo by Scott Grey of Carpinteria, Calif.

Going for a bath in the kitchen sink—Gabriel Beauchamp Kelley, 11 months, assisted by his mother, Jan Beauchamp of Juneau, Alaska. Photo by Mark Kelley of Juneau, Jan's husband and Gabriel's father.

► ►

On following page: One-month-old Ryan Wilde on the Desolation Trail at Kilauea Volcano, Hawaii. Photo by his father, John H. Wilde of Santa Clara, Calif.

◄

Missy Noblett, 20, and her daughter, Britney, 16 months, gaze at wheat field in Texas. Photo by Terry G. Savage of Amarillo, Tex.

Five Mennonite girls watch the world go by on ferry from Cape May, N.J., to Lewes, Del. Photo by Nancy Cohen of Lisle, Ill.

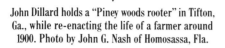

John Dillard holds a "Piney woods rooter" in Tifton, Ga., while re-enacting the life of a farmer around 1900. Photo by John G. Nash of Homosassa, Fla.

▶

Amish family in Lancaster County, Pa. Photo by Roxanne L. Dill of Franklinton, La.

▲

A tire makes a resting place for Joe Redington, 10, and kitten in Butler County, Kan. Photo by Michelle Redington of Towanda, Kan.

◄

It's no big deal. Four-year-old Michael Czechowskyj brings his first catch back to Big Star Lake Campground, near Baldwin, Mich. Photo by his mother, Marianne Czechowskyj of Allendale, Mich.

On a windy day at the Grand Canyon, Jones Benally, a Navajo medicine man,
demonstrates for his son how to pose at the canyon's edge. Photo by Geri Moore of Winter Haven, Fla.

Sunrise in Grand Central Terminal in New York City.
Photo by Charles F. Jennes of Norwalk, Conn.

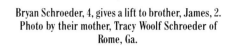

Bryan Schroeder, 4, gives a lift to brother, James, 2. Photo by their mother, Tracy Woolf Schroeder of Rome, Ga.

Cousins. From left to right: Bixby Cooper, 6; David Cooper 8; David Walters, 13; Michael Walters, 11; and Lewis Cooper, 10. Bixby died of cancer six months after this photo was taken. Photo by Kent Walters of Atlanta, Ga.

► Company "A" of the 19th Tennessee Volunteer Infantry at Chickamauga and Chattanooga National Military Park. L-r: Lt. Joseph Mays, Cpl. Monty Elfgen, Pvt. John Sanders, Pvt. Dale Chambers, Pvt. Tony Cordell, Pvt. Tim Hickey. Photo by Frank O'Rear of Sioux City, Iowa.

◄◄ On previous page, The skirts of Liberty. Photo by Joanie Sabler of Sarasota, Fla.

Talk of the town. June Champlin, left, confers
with Sydney Dobbs, moderator, at annual town
meeting in Cushing, Maine. Photo by Stephen
Heddericg of Camden, Maine.

66 *God must love the common man;*
he made so many of them. **99**

—Abraham Lincoln

66 *The genius of the United States is not*
best or worst in its
executives or legislators, nor its ambassadors or authors
or colleges or churches or parlors, nor even its newspapers or monuments…
but always most in the common people. **99**

—Walt Whitman

66 *The Consitution does not provide for*
first and second class citizens. **99**

—Wendell Wilkie

66 *I think if the people of this country*
can be reached with the truth, their judgment will be in favor of the many,
as against the privileged few. **99**

—Eleanor Roosevelt, quoted in *The Ladies Home Journal*, May 1942

66 *We are concerned not only about the Negro poor,*
but the poor all over America and all over the world.
Every man deserves a right to a job or
an income so that he can pursue liberty, life, and happiness. **99**

—Coretta Scott King

66 *Ask not what your country can do for you;*
ask what you can do for your country. **99**

—John F. Kennedy

66 *Do what you can,*
with what you have, where you are. **99**

—Theodore Roosevelt

▶
Flags stand furled in
foyer of old Lake County
Courthouse in Crown
Point, Ind. Photo by
Robert D. Beard of
Steger, Ill.

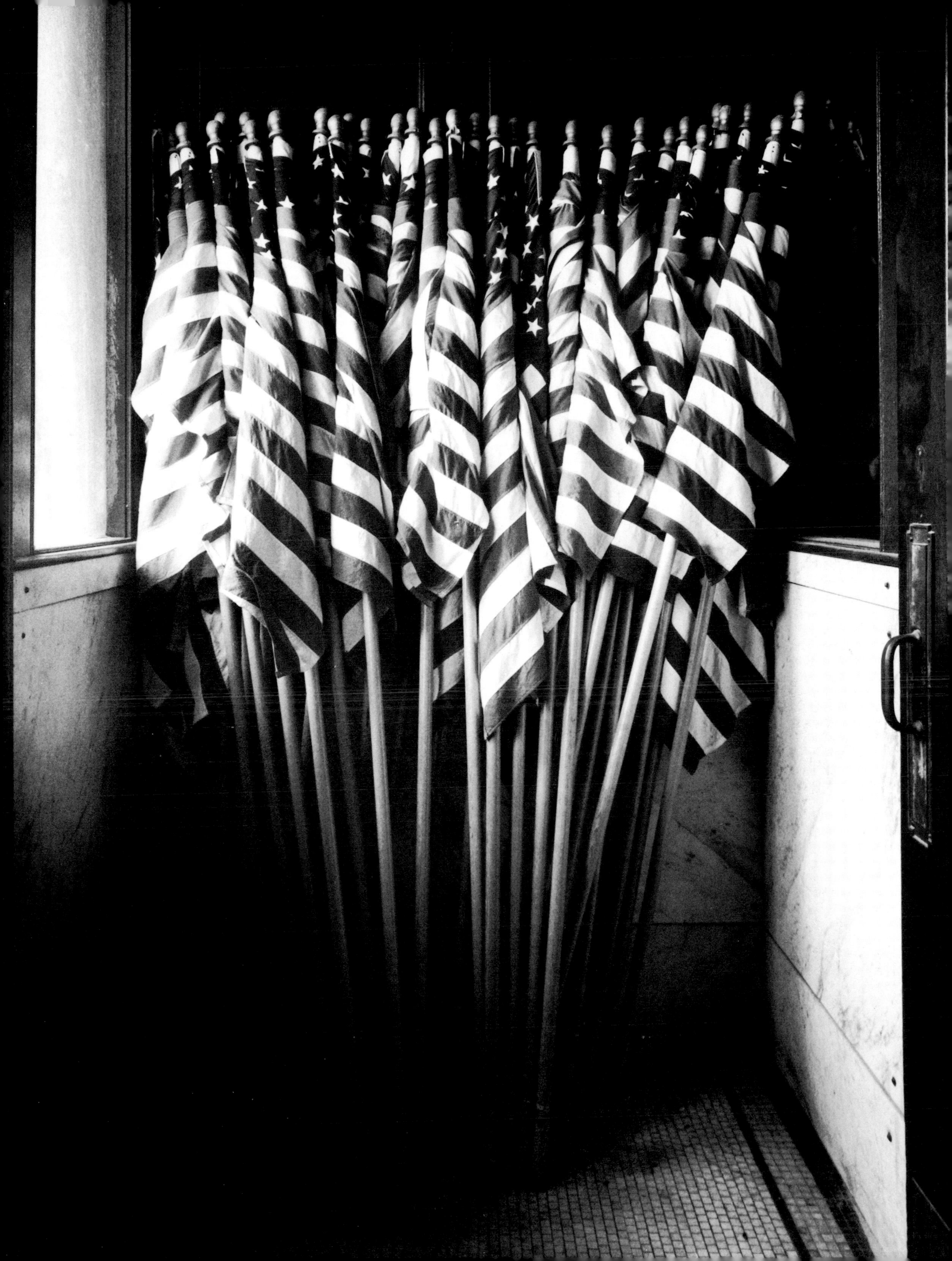

▶

Hey there! Two-year-old Ashley May gets a smile
from Grandma, Frances May, on ranch near Jackson
Hole, Wyo. Photo by Lorraine C. May, Ashley's mother,
of South Beach, Ore.

▲

Fifth Street Jukebox. Photo taken in Santa Rosa, Calif.,
by Aron L. Campisano of Santa Rosa.

▶
Evening, July 4,
Jacksonville, Fla. Photo
by Judy K. Jacobsen of
Jacksonville.

◀◀
On previous page. Three
generations of the Powell
family on the beach in
Gearhart, Ore. Photo by
Owen Carey of Portland,
Ore.

▶▶
On following page: The
Mt. Nebo Methodist
Church in Delta, Pa.
Photo by Maurice L. Kief
of Whiteford, Md.

Father and daughter. Stephen Eyraud, 44, holds hands with his daughter Simone, 6, in Los Angeles. Photo by Ayn Plant of Riverside, R.I.

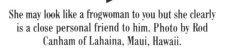

She may look like a frogwoman to you but she clearly is a close personal friend to him. Photo by Rod Canham of Lahaina, Maui, Hawaii.

Tim Waterfall, 31, of Cheyenne descent, is a trail guide on McDowell Mountain Range in Arizona. Photo by Sandra Howard Mazur of Phoenix, Ariz.

Just playing around. Veronica Magri, 2, with mom's makeup kit. Photo by Ronnie's grandfather, Charles W. O'Brien of Staten Island, N.Y.

Hey, kid! Bry Ewan of Georgetown, Tex., has a look around during session at baseball camp. Photo by David Sprague of Austin, Tex.

Afternoon at Long Beach, N.Y. Stroller with cane on
porch of retirement home. Photo by Gary L. Brody of Freeport, N.Y.

▶
Where is everybody? A doleful Rand Hall Jr., 16 months, stares out the door of his home. Photo by his mother, Janice Chatburn Hall of Methuen, Mass.

▲
Claude Finchum, 84, of Martinsville, Ind., peers out at the land he has farmed for 50 years. Photo by Maureen Kay Treece of Walton, Ky.

Brody Burks, 3, waits for Texas State Railroad to get rolling. Photo by his father, Jim Burks of Granbury, Tex.

▲

The family of Margaret Pelissier, 37, has been running this Marquette, Mich., grocery store since 1921. Photo by Christine Saari of Marquette.

▶

Eugene Jansing says his store in Westphalia, Tex., is combination grocery store, bar, pool hall, feed store and rural hangout—"a place time forgot but we didn't." Photo by Don Tremain of Dallas.

► Kenneth Hattrup, 31, attempts to snap his 2-year-old daughter, Rita, in the spring of 1959 with Rolleiflex camera he bought during the Korean War. Photo by Marie Hattrup, Kenneth's wife and Rita's mother, of The Dalles, Ore.

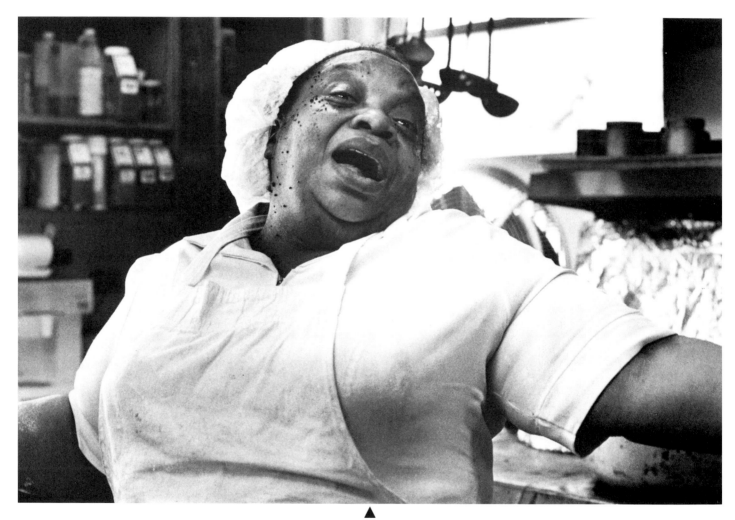

Joy of Cooking. Clementine "Tina" Hawkins in her kitchen at Edison Park Home for troubled adolescents in
Park Ridge, Ill. Photo by Jo Ann Brandner Dollar of Evanston, Ill.

Flour Power. Margaret Lucas, 26, is a baker at Life Experiences, an organization in Cary, N.C., operated by the mentally handicapped. Photo by Lisa M. Stroud of Apex, N.C.

The new West: Erin Graham, 20, wrangles horses at Grand Teton National Park in Wyoming. Photo by Mary Alice Webber of St. Paul, Minn.

▲
Mark this one "Fragile." Katie Calhoun, 2, waits for the mailman.
Photo by her father, Michael F. Calhoun of Santa Barbara, Calif.

▶
Another world. Johna Stoltzfuss, an Amish boy, rides a
horse-drawn buggy on a Lancaster, Pa., road.
Photo by Jeffrey L. Hixon of Wrightsville, Pa.

Benjamin Allan Smith, 1, gets his first clipping from Jack Crone, 35, at Days Barbershop in Atlanta, Ga. Photo by Ben's mother, Alice H. Smith of Atlanta.

On previous page, Daniel Lowe, 19, waterskis on shimmering Priest Lake, Idaho, on an early August morning. Photo by Lee McClellan of Seattle, Wash.

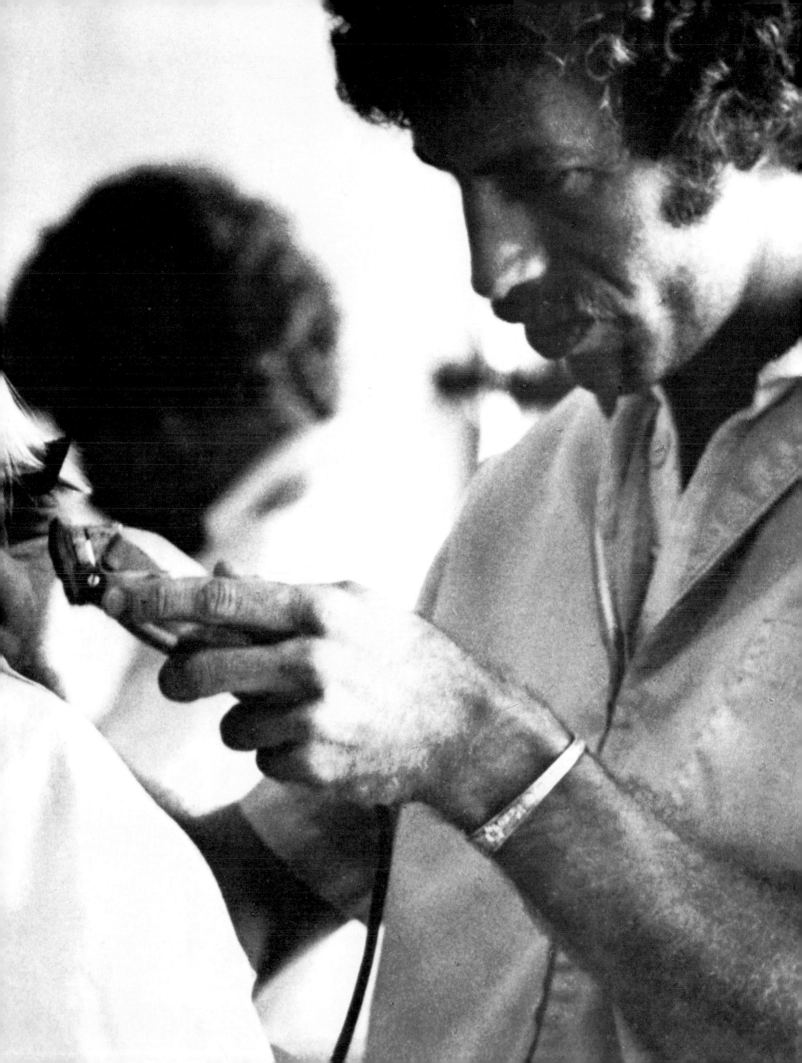

Skateboarder. He's holding it in his hand while he shows off on a boardwalk in Seaside Heights, N.J. Photo by Gerard P. Byrne of Washington, D.C.

Caroline Corwin, 18 months, goes exploring on her grandparents' farm in Beaufort, N.C., and discovers a friendly face. Photo by her mother, Gail Edwards Corwin of Beaufort, N.C.

Catch the rays. Adam Bennett Helton, 6 months old, takes a sunbath along Oak Creek in Sedona, Ariz. Photo by his mother, Caroline Helton of Mesa, Ariz.

▲
William Jeremiah Hunt, born 1899: Court crier,
Oconee County Courthouse, Walhalla, S.C. Photo by
William L. Dodson Jr. of Greenville, S.C.

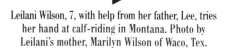
Leilani Wilson, 7, with help from her father, Lee, tries
her hand at calf-riding in Montana. Photo by
Leilani's mother, Marilyn Wilson of Waco, Tex.

Allan L. Stewart of McConnelsville, Ohio, breeder of prizewinning Shropshire sheep.
Photo by his son-in-law, Walter A. Jones of Spring Hill, Tenn.

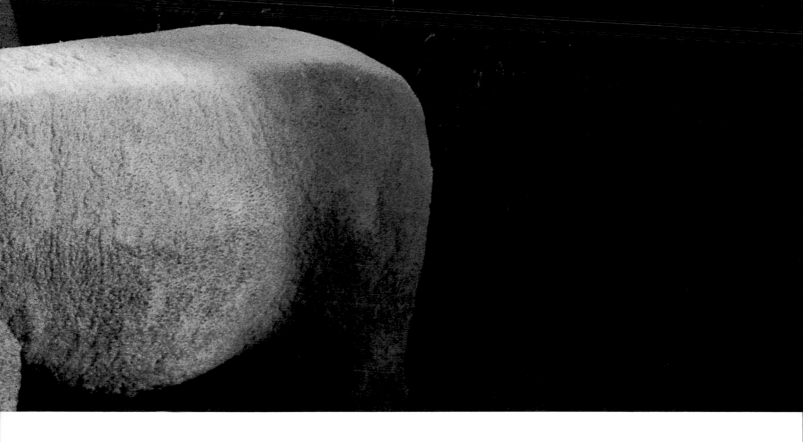

▲

Nat LaPadura, sculptor of fine art and designer of toys, in front of workbench in Bradley Beach, N.J., studio. Photo by Brian W. Michels of Jackson, N.J.

◀

Big hands guide little ones through pottery-making session at a Renaissance Festival in Carver, Mass. Photo by Gail Rosensweig of Wareham, Mass.

Ike Ward, a former slave aged 118, quenches his thirst in Seville, Fla. Photo by Matthew J. Altenbach of Millcreek, Fla.

Blossoms in springtime. Jason McKinley, 9, and his sister, Amber, 6, in bluebonnet field near Austin, Tex. Photo by their mother, Cecily McKinley of Austin.

Ring-bearer Rocky Shore, 4, squires flower girl Jenny Herd, also 4, at a relative's wedding. Photo by Tony Shore of Baltimore, Md.

Oscar, 84, and Lottie
Puckett, 83, married 60
years, have 24
great-grandchildren.
Photo by Don
Etheridge-Davis of
Woodstock, Ga.

On following page.
Things are bubbling up
for Jennifer McCurdy, 3,
in Atlanta.
Photo by Julia Dinkins
of Avondale Estates, Ga.

▲

John Michael Gunderman is happily at home amid plastic bubbles in an Anaheim, Calif., amusement park.
Photo by John's mother, Kim Gunderman of Indianapolis, Ind.

▲

Lesley Mariko Graves, 3, takes a head-first slide. Photo
by Phillip Shelton of Manhattan Beach, Calif.

119

▶
President and Mrs.
Reagan comfort families
of *U.S.S. Stark*
casualties. Photo by
James-Michael Roddy of
Atlantic Beach, Fla.

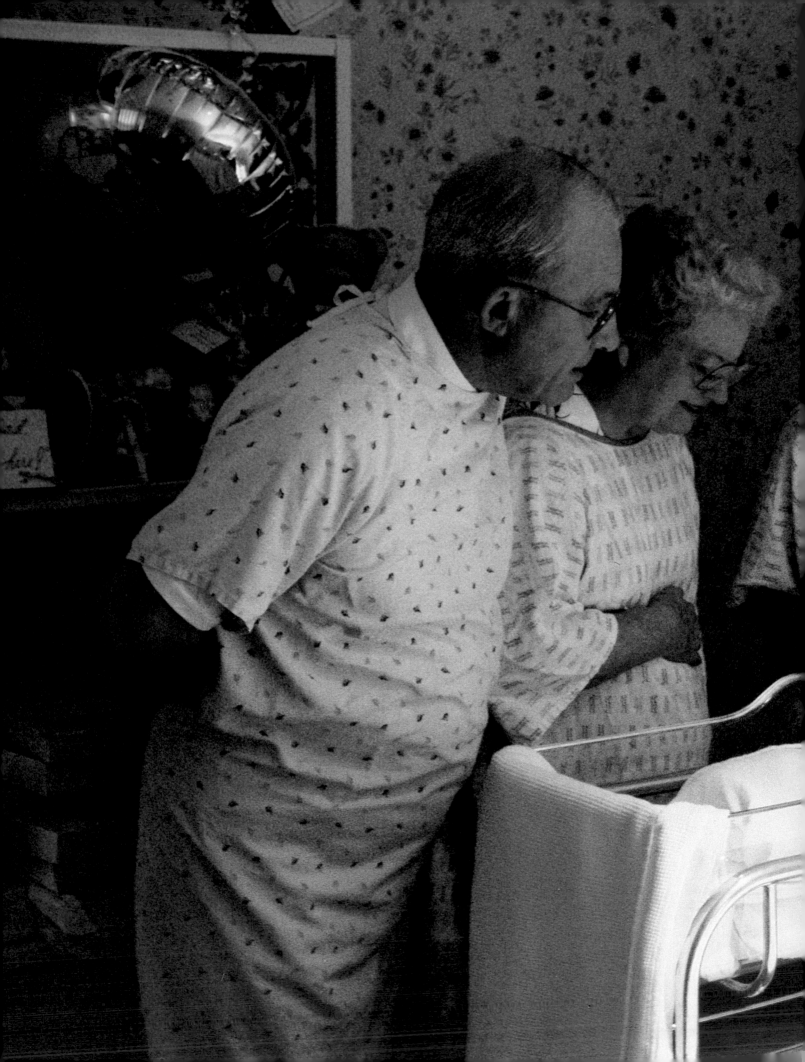

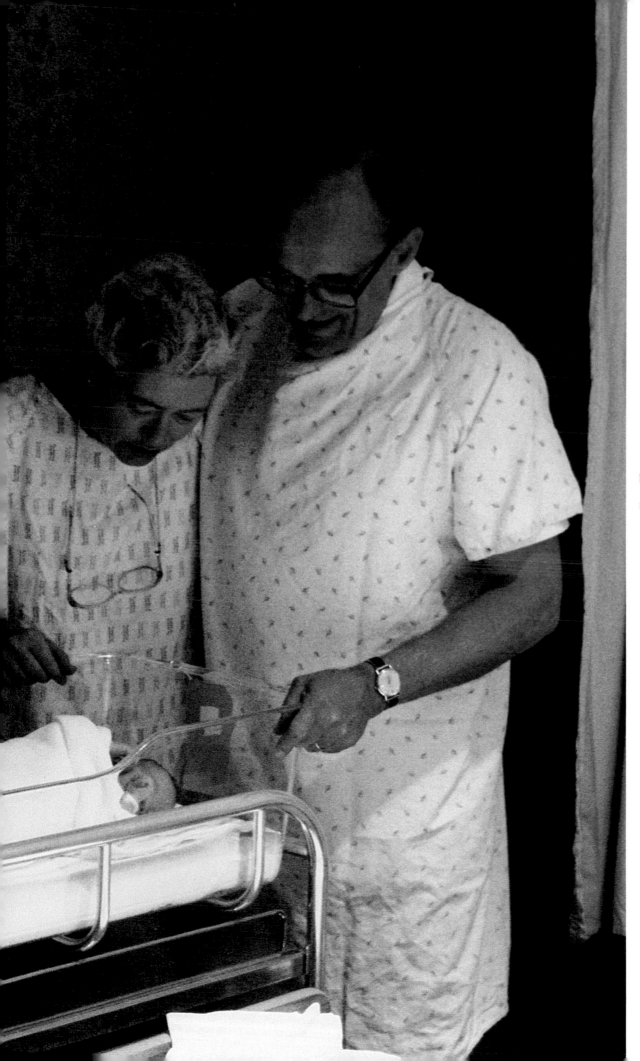

All four grandparents of 2-day-old Jonathan Richard Dreasler await their turn to hold the new arrival at Blessing Hospital in Quincy, Ill. From left: John and Elaine Dreasler, Mae and Dick Shierling. Photo by Brady W. Dreasler of Quincy.

►►

On following page. With a self-timer, the photographer captures himself near an 1887 gravesite in Southbury, Conn., on a morning in March. Photo by John R.D. Lucvinko of Woodbury, Conn.

123

▲

Ethel Craven, 81, who lives four blocks from the street she was born
on in Roslyn, Wash., has "more grandchildren and great-grandchildren
than I can count." Photo by Barbara J. Witt of Seattle.

▲

Teachers Glayde J. Moore and Bud Cudmore grin and bare it during the Northshore School
District's Fifth Grade Campout on Whidbey Island, Wash. (Word is the kids loved it.) Photo by
a fellow schoolteacher, Judy Fawcett of Bothell, Wash.

At the end of the day.
The beach at Santa
Barbara, Calif. Photo by
Dan Burkholder of Santa
Barbara.

► Claire Younker, 13, with her registered quarterhorse mare, Ima Elegant Cash, or "Elly" for short. Photo by Claire's mother, Linda Quartman Younker of Bainbridge Island, Wash.

▲ Seaman Michael Marino and wife, Kelly, share a welcome-home kiss aboard the *U.S.S. Kinkaid.* Marino had just returned stateside from an eight-month tour in the South Pacific and Middle East. Photo by his brother, Robert J. Marino of Staten Island, N.Y.

▶
Sean Michael Macaulay, 2, catches bubbles at sunset. Photo by his cousin, Christiana Kurzhals of Norwood, Mass.

▶ ▶
On following page. Flags and people were gathered at Mt. Tamalpais in Marin County, California, for a chewing gum commercial. Photo by Shirley Anne Richards of San Pedro.

132

▶
Fourth of July
tug-of-war in Felton,
Calif. Photo by Bill
Dunniway of Mount
Hermon, Calif.

❝ *Whatever else an American believes or disbelieves about himself, he is absolutely sure he has a sense of humor.* **❞**

—E. B. White

❝ *The American people never carry an umbrella. They prepare to walk in eternal sunshine.* **❞**

—Alfred E. Smith

❝ *There are five of my people playing for the Boston Celtics, and the Irish people love it. Someday there's going to be a team called Black Power, and there'll be five white guys dribbling up the court.* **❞**

—Bill Cosby

❝ *The happy ending is our national belief.* **❞**

—Mary McCarthy

◀

Kelly Young-Wolff, 3, and
her brother, Colin, 5,
salute the sunset at a
park near their home.
Photo by their father,
David S. Young-Wolff of
Santa Monica, Calif.

I was amazed at the diversity of these photographs, all of which spelled "America" to me. The pictures made graphically clear something I've always felt about America—that we really are a diverse melting pot, we really are brothers and sisters— not that that means we have to be twins!

One of the most important things to me is a sense of humor, and it was a joy to see it in these pictures. Life can get grim at times for most of us, but it's amazing to me how little sadness there is in this collection. Most Americans are optimistic, with a sense of joy, and their qualities shine through these pictures.

And there is also a great sense of family history. People used to keep their family record written in their bibles, but today it's more likely to be remembered in still photos of how we were, where we are, and where we're going. These pictures enable us to live for a few moments in other people's lives—very important at a time when many family ties are loosening.

In the past, when you got married, you took a piece of the family farm and lived down the road and you could always go back to grandma or your grandfather for some wisdom or understanding. But today grandma may be clinging to a telephone pole for a company in San Diego and grandpa may be doing puts and calls on Wall Street, so you don't have this sense of past and present and future, the continuity we used to have. But these pictures give us that, some of the ties we're missing, showing as they do new traditions, old traditions, a glimpse into other people's lives and wisdom.

And love is the theme of so many of them—all varieties: older people for younger people, younger for older, kids for one another, affection for animals, couples sharing their lives and dreams. This is not ourselves as others see us; this is the way we see ourselves.

Joyce Brothers

There's a great quote by Albert Einstein that says, in effect: People change, but a photograph remains the same; you remember people as they once were.

I think that's so beautiful, because a photographic image is so powerful and flesh is so weak. It's true, a photgraph is just paper and you can tear it easily. Sometimes I go on assignment and I'm shocked by how much it can cost, when you figure in all the expenses, just to make two rolls of film. But then I think of how we live in a world of images, and it doesn't bother me as much.

When you think of the Revolutionary Battle of Yorktown, for example, you think of a painting; when you think of World War II, you think of the photograph of the flag-raising on Iwo Jima; when you think of Vietnam, you think of a front-page picture of a naked child running down the road.

I think every person in the world should own a camera. People used to write letters, but now they talk on the phone and take pictures and those pictures are just about the only record we have of our past. It's interesting to me that, today, there is more respect for a still photo than there ever was.

Photographs fascinate me. Not long ago I was a judge in a big international competition and the first-place photo had been taken with an Instamatic. It was out of focus, blurred even, but it showed these two little kids all dressed up for a make-believe wedding or something and the little boy had this hilarious, impossibly disgusted look on his face. The whole picture was warm. Everything was so warm in it. Technically it was all wrong but it was beautiful and it won 10,000 dollars.

A lot of times people ask me how to learn to take pictures and I say to them get all the books on all the technical things, read them, learn the basics, then throw the books away and do the opposite of everything they tell you.

Put together a darkroom and shoot black and white, which is coming back now too. It's more difficult to shoot black and white than it is color because the color can take over and make even a lousy photo look good, whereas black and white, a good black-and-white photo, has a power that lasts a lot longer than color. So I say get black and white down, and then play with color film.

I am asked about when to take pictures too and, as I think most people know, the hour at sunrise and the hour at sunset are far and away the best times to shoot, unless the day is overcast. Then you can shoot anytime. But avoid noon or anytime the sun is high because you get a flat picture. When the light is lower, in the morning or evening, you get a roundness and form that give shape to your picture.

I also believe you should always, or most of the time, try to get a person in your picture. People come first, nature second, because human beings are the most important thing in the world. I've always believed this and felt that it was obvious.

People change, but a photograph remains the same. In my judgment, a good photograph does not have to be technically excellent. If it makes you laugh or cry or evokes an emotional response, then I think it is a good photograph.

The pictures in *Parade*'s "We The People Contest" did just that: some made me laugh, some made me cry. They are real pictures of real people.

Eddie Adams

When our nation celebrated the Bicentennial of the Constitution, I often thought about the many aspects of the American people and our government that are unique. One important aspect of the American psyche, embodied in the Constitution, is the idea of character. James Madison believed that our rights are not defined on paper, but are safeguarded in the habits and institutions, i.e. character, of the American people. Philosopher Michael Novak has said that "character is necessary to release the spiritual energy for self-government...to release that energy, a society needs persons of character, who are able to make decisions for themselves, to take responsibility for themselves, to bear risk and loss, and of course *and above all*, to know how to work with others."

This decade has shown a tremendous resurgence of the idea of character and its essential contribution to the survival of our country. Nowhere is this more evident than in the photographs I judged for *Parade* magazine. In virtually every photograph, the message of national character—respect for life and traditional values of family, individual accomplishment, and community—was a common theme.

As the Director of the Federal Domestic Volunteer Agency, ACTION, I have had the extraordinary opportunity of traveling around the country to visit America's volunteers who, in the words of Novak, "know how to work with others." I have gained an appreciation for the diversity of our people and how each individual contributes to the whole of our unique national character. I found this diversity reflected in almost every photograph I judged.

The difficult task was, of course, choosing 100 photographs from the many entries. The photographs were extraordinary in their range of subject matter. My overwhelming impression of the group was the ease of expression, the sense of openness exhibited by the subjects. I often hear foreign visitors remark that Americans communicate more freely and are less reserved than other people. This warm and human quality permeated the photographs and made selection extremely difficult.

The photographs I chose will, I hope, reach the individual viewer at the deepest level and stir a sense of the common experience. Many of these photographs communicate forceful messages of freedom, strength, and optimism. But some recall memories of family and hometown experiences that may be all but forgotten for some Americans. In these challenging times, they will evoke the traditions and values of our people which are so critical to instill in America's youth.

I am pleased to be associated with a project that shows the strength, character, and freedom of the American people through such a forceful visual medium. As we continue to reflect on the blessings of liberty following the Bicentennial year, these photographs will endure as a reminder that a most remarkable feature of our culture is that there is indeed unity in our diversity.

Donna M. Alvarado

Any national photographic contest that is open to all comers inevitably will produce what amounts to a mirror of not only the faces but also of the spirits or, one might even say, of the "flavor" of the populace of that country. This has been impressed upon me most powerfully as a result of my taking part in the judging of the entries for *Parade* magazine's "We The People Photo Contest," which was the basis for this book.

As I thumbed through stacks and stacks of photos, sorting out one after another with great reluctance—there were so many I liked so well and I hated to put them down but I *had* to make choices—I thought a number of times about a trip I made to an Iron Curtain country and about the pictures I had seen at a photo exhibit there. The country had recently held a contest similar to *Parade's* and all the photos were on display and the hosts beamed with pride at their cultural display. But the pictures were formal and postured, and the faces were staring and those that were smiling seemed to do so with uncertainty.

How different were these I was judging! They were faces, old and young and in-between, of an unfettered people, free and open and, it was clear, unafraid of taking chances.

These photographs frequently all but sang with their spontaneous laughter and happiness and gaiety. Even solemn elders often reflected a twinkle. I was, I am, very moved when I reflect that what I have "judged" is the buoyant face of America.

Alex Haley

▲

Navajo woman, Monument Valley, Ariz., summer 1986.
Photo by Kevin T. Pate of Chandler, Ariz.